"NOW FOR MY NEXT TRICK..."

Published as a trade paperback original
by Alyson Publications, 40 Plympton St., Boston, Mass. 02118.
Distributed in the U.K. by GMP Publishers,
PO Box 247, London, N15 6RW, England.

First edition: December, 1986

ISBN 1-55583-101-X

"Now For My Next Trick..."

Cartoons from The Washington Blade

by
Michael Willhoite

Boston : Alyson Publications, Inc.

To Judy

"KY, Vaseline, Crisco
. . . Give me good
old-fashioned slime
any day."

6

"GM, hot, horny, hairy.
Desires same..."

7

"His work made a definite turnaround in the late sixties — What does 'Stonewall' mean, anyway?"

9

"I'm sorry, Don, but when something's over, it's over! Besides, you've run out of cavities."

"Dear Reverend Falwell —
We senators have always
kissed babies to get
elected. Your insistence on
knowing the ratio of boy
to girl babies is an insult
and furthermore . . ."

"I can't get over how they
flaunt their sexuality."

13

"Oh, no, Larry —
only girls can grow up to
be queens."

"Son, when you're through coming out can I have my gloves back?"

15

"I don't know what it's about, but at least it's got sexy showgirls!"

"Son, you do mean 'merry and bright,' don't you?"

17

"I'm glad you enjoyed this scene, Elaine, but I feel I should tell you I'm a much better actor than you think."

"Why, my son's coming-out party was even more fun than my daughter's!"

"Sure, I can tell them fags a mile off — any real man can!"

20

"Tall and . . . Something . . . Hair . . . Something . . . Something . . . Desires same . . ."

"I can assure you that we're not *concerned* with closet space."

22

"He's very possessive."

23

"My roommates are straight . . . but very understanding."

"I'm not bisexual, but I have strayed from the gay and narrow a couple of times."

Man secure in the knowledge that he'll never have to come up with a great opening line again.

"Now for my next trick..."

27

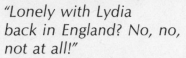

"Lonely with Lydia
back in England? No, no,
not at all!"

28

"Barry! You've marched in Selma! You worked for Chavez! You resisted the draft in '68 — and you're afraid your mother will see you on television?!"

"*I'd go straight first.*"

"God, how butch can you get!"

31

"Brad's NOT seeing another woman? But shouldn't that make you happy?"

"I hate to think of you out on the prairie with nothing but Indian squaws for companionship."

"'Good,' Alexander? Why, you were great!"

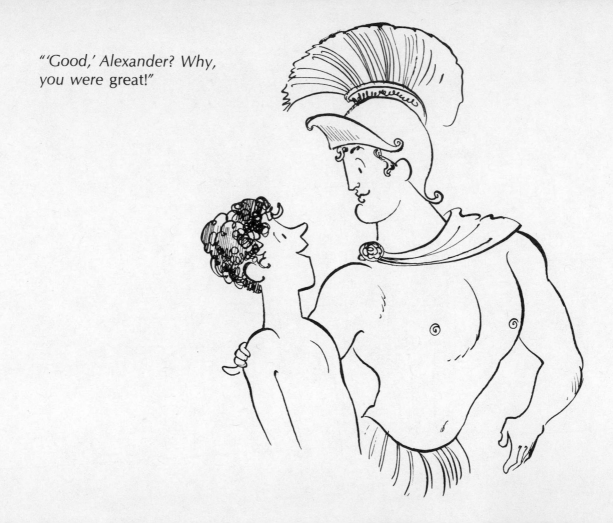

"Tell me, Sappho,
is there someone else?"

"Stop worrying, Casanova — who'd believe it anyway?"

"That Attila!! Just who does she think she's fooling?"

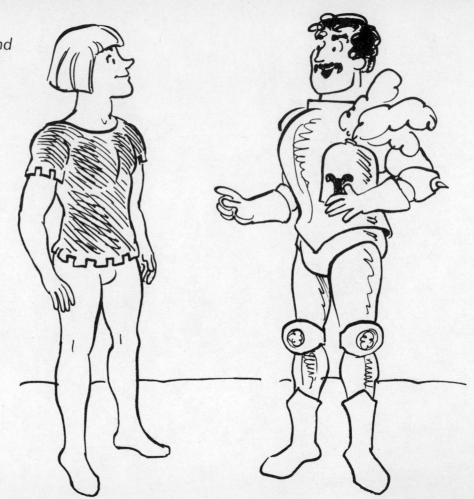

"As my squire, you'll find you have a few, er, unusual duties."

"Sorry — you should have asked!"

39

"Oh, Oscar . . . another night out with the boys?"

40

"Dear Watson — I've found something better than cocaine and the violin combined...!"

"Oh, come on Franz, you can finish your symphony later."

"They're cracking down on
everybody, Babycakes!"

43

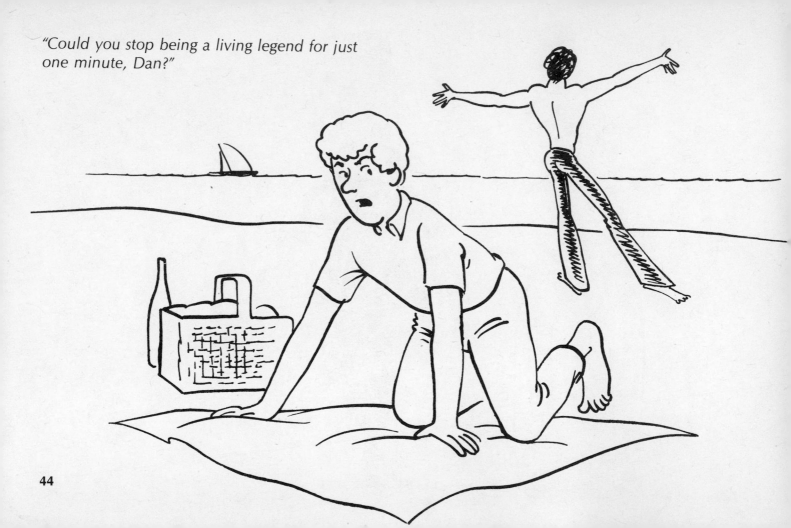

"Could you stop being a living legend for just one minute, Dan?"

44

"A Liza Minnelli record, light beer, poppers, Frye boots; what's this spell for anyway?!"

"No, Hal, you've got to be more cool about it!"

"It's a small place, but I've made it mine."

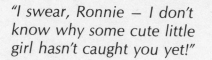

"I swear, Ronnie — I don't know why some cute little girl hasn't caught you yet!"

50

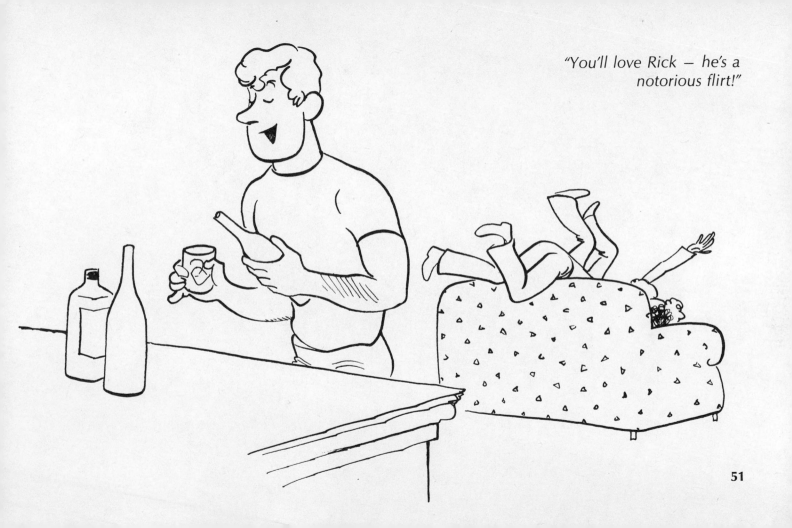

"You'll love Rick — he's a notorious flirt!"

"Look, I just can't help it —
drag makes me uncomfortable!"

"We're in luck!"

53

"Well, Harvey, we can only hope they're just chubby chasers."

"Do you come here often?"

55

"I say, Calthorpe, get your hand off my knee — I understand this tribe is notoriously intolerant of homosexuality."

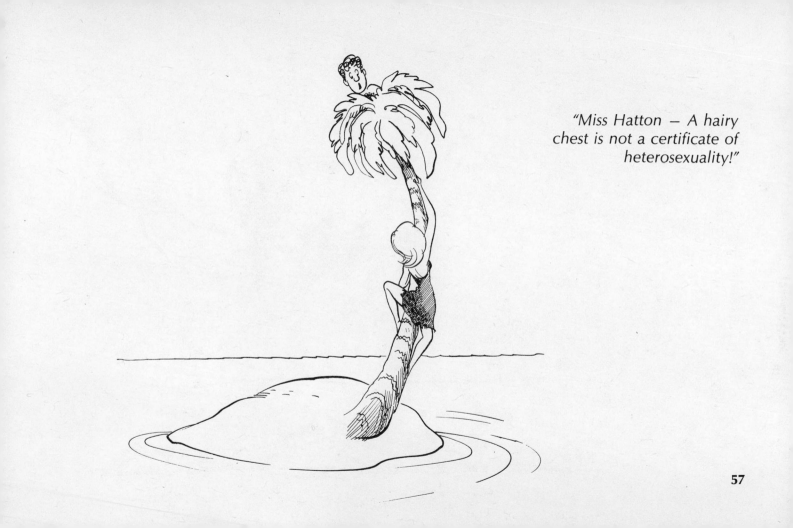

"Miss Hatton — A hairy chest is not a certificate of heterosexuality!"

"Whaddaya mean — you're waiting for someone young and hunky?!"

58

"Now, who had the Brandy Alexander?"

"Reynolds is still under your car but I don't know how long he'll be . . ."

60

*"Well, I figured,
everybody has poodles."*

61

"Wow! An escort service that really delivers the goods!"

63

"Well, Cheetah, one of us has to tell her . . ."

65

"*Perhaps I'd better explain, ma'am . . .*"

"Your courage is remarkable, Richard, but we feel the governor's gay liaison should be a bit more sedate."

"...And they are having so much fun!"

THIS WEEK:
THE LAVENDER PERIL

"Well, Mom — your child who was born on the Sabbath day is blithe and bonny and good and guess what."

"Richardson, making Chiquita banana a lesbian is not what I call going for the gay market!"

"Homosexuality is hereditary and present to some extent in everyone."
—Dr. Christian Bernard

"Must be that time of month again . . ."

"Homosexuals thrive on danger."
— Dr. David Reuben

"Bug off, Mary!"

"I believe, when an individual prefers a member of his (or her) own sex as an object of physical love, that person suffers from a severe personality disorder."

— Ann Landers

"A little strange, maybe . . . but gay — NEVER!!!"

74

"So you still think your parents don't accept me after last night?"

"Oh, that reminds me —
did you remember to
borrow Larry and Bob's
punchbowls for the party?"

"Of course he is! How many straight men have that much style?"

79

A teenage boy who once thought he was 'the only one in the world' arrives at P Street Beach on Gay Pride Day.

"Just out, huh?"

"Darling, did I ever tell you anything about my years at sea?"

82

"But your ad didn't say you were into dominance!"

"Not your typical shipboard romance — but what the hell!"

Broadway, on the night a homophobic star wished there were no gays in the American theater.

"Now why would Mr. Reardon want 'God Save the Queen' sung at his funeral?"

"Mr. Shakespeare, I just don't think that sonnets written to another man have any literary merit."

"A pink squirrel!
Is nothing sacred?!"

THE IRON STUD

88

"I just wonder what kind of cake the Gay Democrats got."

"Well, the new neighbors definitely aren't *sisters!*"

"Actually, I always pictured it as being more like Provincetown."

"Son, this girlfriend that moved out for our visit . . . She, uh, left something behind."

Other books of interest from ALYSON PUBLICATIONS

☐ **THE MEN WITH THE PINK TRIANGLE,** by Heinz Heger, $6.00. In a chapter of gay history that is only recently coming to light, thousands of homosexuals were thrown into the Nazi concentration camps along with Jews and others who failed to fit the Aryan ideal. There they were forced to wear a pink triangle so that they could be singled out for special abuse. Most perished. Heger is the only one ever to have told his full story.

☐ **REFLECTIONS OF A ROCK LOBSTER: A story about growing up gay,** by Aaron Fricke, $6.00. When Aaron Fricke took a male date to the senior prom, no one was surprised: he'd gone to court to be able to do so, and the case had made national news. Here Aaron tells his story, and shows what gay pride can mean in a small New England town.

☐ **ONE TEENAGER IN TEN: Writings by gay and lesbian youth,** edited by Ann Heron, $4.00. One teenager in ten is gay; here, twenty-six young people tell their stories: of coming to terms with being different, of the decision how — and whether — to tell friends and parents, and what the consequences were.

☐ **THE MOVIE LOVER,** by Richard Friedel, $7.00. The entertaining coming-out story of Burton Raider, who is so elegant that as a child he reads *Vogue* in his playpen. "The writing is fresh and crisp, the humor often hilarious," writes the *L.A. Times.*

☐ **EIGHT DAYS A WEEK,** by Larry Duplechan, $7.00. Can Johnnie Ray Rousseau, a 22-year-old black singer, find happiness with Keith Keller, a six-foot-two blond bisexual jock who works in a bank? Will Johnnie Ray's manager ever get him on the Merv Griffin show? Who was the lead singer of the Shangri-las? And what about Snookie? Somewhere among the answers to these and other silly questions is a love story as funny, and sexy, and memorable, as any you'll ever read.

☐ **THE TWO OF US,** by Larry Uhrig, $7.00. The author draws on his years of counseling with gay people to give some down-to-earth advice about what makes a relationship work. He gives special emphasis to the religious aspects of gay unions.

☐ **THE LAVENDER COUCH,** by Marny Hall, $8.00. Here is a guide to the questions that should be considered by lesbians or gay men considering therapy or already in it: How do you choose a good therapist? What kind of therapy is right for you? When is it time to leave therapy?

☐ **SECOND CHANCES,** by Florine de Veer, $7.00. Is it always harder to accept what is offered freely? Jeremy, who is just coming out, could easily have the love of his devoted friend Roy, yet he chooses to pursue the handsome and unpredictable Mark instead.

☐ **DANCER DAWKINS AND THE CALIFORNIA KID,** by Willyce Kim, $6.00. Dancer Dawkins would like to just sit back and view life from behind a pile of hotcakes. But her lover, Jessica Riggins, has fallen into the clutches of Fatin Satin Aspen, and something must be done. Meanwhile, Little Willie Gutherie of Bangor, Maine, renames herself The California Kid, stocks up on Rubbles Dubble bubble gum, and heads west. When this crew collides in San Francisco, what can be expected? Just about anything. . . .

☐ **CHOICES,** by Nancy Toder, $8.00. This popular novel about lesbian love depicts the joy, passion, conflicts and intensity of love between women as Nancy Toder conveys the fear and confusion of a woman coming to terms with her sexual and emotional attraction to other women.